GOD LIVES IN MIRACLES

By

Judith Hester

Copyright © 2010 by Judith M. Hester

God Lives In Miracles
by Judith M. Hester

Printed in the United States of America

ISBN 9781612150178

All rights reserved solely by the author. The author guarantees all contents are original and do not infringe upon the legal rights of any other person or work. No part of this book may be reproduced in any form without the permission of the author. The views expressed in this book are not necessarily those of the publisher.

Unless otherwise indicated, Bible quotations are taken from The King James Version of the Bible; and The New King James Version. Copyright © 1990 by Thomas Nelson Publishers, used by permission.

www.xulonpress.com

TABLE OF CONTENTS

1. The God of the Supernatural 11
2. Understanding Divine Order 18
3. His Name Is Jesus 23
4. The First Key—Intimacy with the Holy Spirit 27
5. God's Design for Miracles 31
6. The Second Key—The Prophetic Vessel 45
7. Understanding the Process 57
8. The Third Key—the Lifestyle of Prayer 61
9. Dwelling in the Supernatural 73
10. Endnotes 79

To my husband, Ezra,

For more than twenty years

To my children,

For showing me the value of parenting

TO THE READER

Given a mandate to write *God Lives in Miracles* more than ten years ago, it has been a book birthed out of heartfelt experiences and travail. This book is written for the Christian who desires a serious and closer walk with God and to the unbeliever who needs to be introduced to an ever-loving Savior. God cares for you, and whatever it is that you are experiencing in your life He will bring you through it. This book tells you how.

Life's experiences have taken me on a wondrous journey of discovering God's design and purpose for my life.

It is my prayer that those with a prophetic mandate and calling will glean from the richness of my experience. Over the years I have learned at the feet of some of the world's most renowned men and women of faith. Their lives have been the inspiration which has helped to propel me into divine destiny, and it is the leading and teaching of the Holy Spirit which has guided me through the daily occurrences of life. This is where the true nuggets are found. I have come to understand that both triumphs and tragedies are all orchestrated by the hand of God to mature and equip the believer for God's purposes. This book is meant for you to see your life through heaven's perspective.

Exploring the supernatural for the believer releases the power of God in a dimension of limitless possibilities.

He is indeed a good God. I hope that you will begin to experience the miraculous working dimension of His limitless abilities as you delight in the revelation that God lives in miracles.

Chapter 1

The God of the Supernatural

"With God all things are possible."
Matthew 19:26

God is a God of the supernatural. Throughout the Scripture His methodology for the advertisement of His divine existence and ability is found in the working of miracles. Yet one may ask, what exactly is a miracle? Is it a miracle when a baby is born or a flower blooms? Often we think something unusual or out of the ordinary is a miracle. Yet its description goes much more into detail than that. W.E. Vine defines a miracle in two parts. The first definition is from the Greek word *dunamis* which means "power, inherent ability." This is the term found in Acts 8:13, Acts 19:1, Galatians 3:5 and Hebrews 2:4. These biblical references demonstrate the unlimited ability of God as He reveals more of His power and might.

The second definition from Vine's is the Greek *semeion,* for "a sign, mark or token." This is used in regard to the demonstration of God's divine authority. These are evidences of God's presence. Several scriptural passages are Luke 23:8, John 3:2 and Acts 6:8.

In this definition the message is clear that its power source and purpose are divine in nature. Therefore a miracle exceeds all human ability and comprehension. The first biblical example of a miraculous work of God is in His divine creation of the universe. The scripture states, "In the beginning God created the heavens and the earth" (Genesis 1:1). God begins the Word with a divine action, the miracle of creation. God's oral voice was used to bring something out of nothing. Speech was the mechanism by which He established the existence of the universe. He also created mankind from the formation of dust and breathing the breath of life into existence.

William M. Taylor, pastor of Broadway Tabernacle Church in New York in the 1800s, defined a miracle as "a work out of the usual sequence of secondary causes and effects which cannot be accounted for by the ordinary operation of those causes, and which is produced by the agency of God through the instrumentality of one who claims to be his representative, and in attestation of the message which he brings." In other words, a miracle could not be attributed to natural sources for its existence; yet God used a living source to display its manifestation.

There are those who believe miracles ceased to exist with the early church, but God's Word continues to be a living, transforming entity of mankind's existence. God's communicated message to mankind is the Bible, which is His inspired Word. The Holy Scriptures are the living expression of a divine God. Authorship of the Bible was by the hand of men, as its contents were given from the heart of God. This is described in the Greek word *theopneutos*—

theo meaning God and *pneu* meaning to breath. From the dawn of time the sovereign Creator breathed life into mankind, and God delighted in all that He made. "So God created man in His image, in the image of God created He him; male and female created He them" (Genesis 1:27). Mankind pleased God as mankind was made in the image and likeness of the God of the universe. Theopneutos is the breath of God that sustains life.

Physical man must breathe air in the atmosphere around us in order to survive. Effortlessly we constantly inspire atmospheric air into our lungs. Through the complex process of inspiration and expiration breathing takes place. Breathing is an exchange of gases. Air containing oxygen is taken into our nostrils and mouth from the surrounding atmosphere. Air then flows into the larynx and trachea and enters tiny tubes in our lungs called bronchioles and then into small balloon-like structures called alveoli. There is a complex process called diffusion which causes the gases to exchange into the alveoli and the surrounding tissues and finally to be circulated through the bloodstream. This is how the body receives oxygenation. Conversely, waste products from the body are removed as byproducts of the body are excreted. This is in the form of carbon dioxide and is exhaled by the lungs. This cycle continues to promote life constantly to the body.

As air is essential for the physiological existence of human beings, there is a spiritual void in the heart of every human being which longs to find meaning and fulfillment.

What a person fills this emptiness with, however, is vital. If the spiritual void is not filled with a personal relationship with God, then it is filled with other things. The longing for God will be filled with something or someone. People can fill the void with seemingly healthy things such as family, relationships, work and sports. Although these interactions are healthy and necessary in an individual's life, they are not to be the priority of one's life. The creator of the universe wants that place for Himself. Other types of unhealthy activities exist as well, such as spiritualism, psychics, mind readers, tarot cards and other occult activities. These activities have a satanic origin, and they compete for the place God should inhabit. One must be very careful to ensure that the source of inspiration is God and God alone.

God desires to be the center of the life of the believer. When a person develops a drive or compulsion to be involved in other activities at the exclusion of a relationship with God problems arise.

In the Old Testament book of Job the author writes these compelling words: "The spirit of God hath made me, and the breath of the Almighty hath given me life" (Job 33:4). As the process of breathing sustains life, the Word of God fills a life with the oxygen of divine ability, thereby fortifying one's existence. Job understood that the essence of life came from a divine God with a divine purpose. As Christians, we must come to know and trust that the Scriptures make great sense as the Bible provides clarity and direction for our lives.

A destination is known as a place to which one travels. The wise traveler knows how to get to his destination. Whether by a global positioning system (GPS) or by manually mapping the path to be taken, the wise traveler plans the way to get to the destination.

The Bible is the time-tested, foolproof, advanced global positioning system of God, giving mankind the course of how to navigate in life. Yet despite this clear and accurate record many people question the supernatural ability of an all-powerful God. Most often debated is the miraculous power of the trinity. Many believe the miracles that occurred in the time of the early church do not exist today. Some believe the Bible is only a book of pleasant stories which have no merit to present-day circumstances.

Despite these speculations many people want to believe in the God of the supernatural. Often, however, the churches in which many people may worship no longer believe in the supernatural work of God outside of the redemptive work of salvation, and so they do not experience a fresh move of God's presence. This is called cessationism, and it is the belief that miracles ceased to exist with the death of the last biblically named apostle.

Another reason is because people may not know how to connect with the supernatural Christ Jesus and how He relates to us. We must honor and revere God and cherish His words. Frances Roberts wrote:

Cherish My Words

O My children obey My words. Do not wander in unbelief and darkness, but let the scripture shine as a light upon thy path. My words shall be life unto thee, for My commandments are given for thy health and for any preservation. They will guard thee from folly and guide thee away from danger.

Hide My commandments in thy heart and make them the law of thy life. Cherish My words and take not lightly the least of them. I have not given them to bind thee, but to bring thee into the life of greatest joy and truest liberty.

I have asked thee to give in order that I may bless you more. I have challenged thee to pray, so that I may respond and help thee. I have asked thee to rejoice in order to keep thee from being swallowed up by anxieties. I have asked thee to be humble, to protect thee from the calamities that fall upon the proud. I have asked thee to forgive so as to make thy heart fit to receive My forgiveness. I have asked thee not to love the world, for I would have thee loosed from unnecessary entanglements and free to follow Me.

Sanctification is accomplished in no one by accident. Learn My rules and put them into practice consistently, if you desire to see progress in the growth of thy soul. Holiness is not a feeling—it is the result of repentance and a serious pursuit of God.

It is imperative that the Christian understand that God is the master designer and Creator of everything. This is the Christian worldview of existence. Nothing exists apart from the God of all creation.

Christianity answers the three questions of existence: 1) Creation—where did mankind come from? 2) The fall—what has gone wrong with the world?

3) Redemption—what can be done to fix it? The answers to these three questions reveal the total truth of mankind's existence on the earth. In our world of postmodernism, secular humanism, moral relativism and more philosophical sources of thought, it is the Christian perspective that has endured the rigors of time in this limited aspect of our eternal existence.

Human beings exist at three levels: spirit, soul and body. According to James Montgomery Boice, our uniqueness and superiority to that of the animal kingdom lie in how God created us. In the book of Genesis we read that we are made "in the image of God" (Genesis 1:26-27). The progression is made from the body (matter) to the soul (personality) to the spirit (life with God-consciousness). This places human beings in a chosen and favored position in God's hierarchy. Mankind has the capacity to acknowledge the presence of two distinct levels of existence. One level is the natural level. Everything that is seen with the natural eye exists at this level: clothes, homes, food and everything associated with the natural man. The second level is the spiritual realm. It is in this unseen realm that the kingdom of God, consisting of the Holy Spirit, angels and creative miracles, exists.

The questions arise, what is a miracle, and why don't we see more of them? Before we explore further about miracles we must first examine the designer of miracles. We need to know more about who Jesus is and who the third person of the trinity is—the Holy Spirit.

Chapter 2

Understanding Divine Order

"So the service of the house of the Lord
was set in order."
2 Chronicles 29:35b, NKJV

God established by divine order. This is quite evident in the book of the beginnings, Genesis. In this work God has clearly demonstrated that order is essential in the framework of creation. The world was spoken into existence and fashioned into being by God. Yet simultaneously the dichotomy of liberty and an unlimited potential are found in Him. He is never restrained by the hands of man or the finiteness of our thinking. Mankind is limited to time and space. He alone is God of everything.

There is a contemporary discussion between creationism and evolution. Yet the evidence speaks loudly for itself: Mankind could not have evolved from apes and primates into the developed creation of the human being. Clearly obvious is the reality that we are made in image of the Intelligent Designer. When God created both man and woman, He made an amazing example of biological engineering with the right myriad of interconnecting systems. The complexities in the design of how the human body works, from the cellular reproduction to the birth of a baby, to the function of the human body, are astonishing to study. Creation is the mark of God's miraculous handiwork.

God designs order in such practical ways. I love spending time in my garden. Every spring I study different floral arrangements via the internet. Once I have a mental picture of what I want my garden to look like I go to my favorite horticultural store and pick out the arrangements of flowers and seeds to plant. I visualize arranging flowers with the various heights, colors and textures. Then I place them in the garden where I want to create the effect of beauty and serenity. The next step is to dig a hole deep enough so that the soil will cover the flowers planted. I love the smell of fresh-turned soil. Often I take my time just to dig my gloved hands into the richness of the soil. There is an exhilarating feeling and such a naturally clean smell in this activity.

My mind often wanders to what it must have been like for God to create all of this: the soil, the plants, the earth, you and I. What humility floods my spirit as I ponder His vast love to make me and place me in an environment complete with everything I would need to survive and thrive. I am reminded of the humanity of all mankind when I read Genesis 2:9: "And out of the ground the Lord God made every tree grow that is pleasant to the sight and good for food. The tree of life was also in the midst of the garden." There is something austere about the beauty and majesty of a sovereign God. This is often much more important than we realize.

James Montgomery Boice lists three attributes of God which are unique to God and to man, and not to animal life. The first is personality. Mankind has feelings and possesses knowledge and a will. The second is morality. This encompasses the ability for freedom and responsibility. The third is spirituality. Mankind was created to be in fellowship with the living God. What an awesome privilege to be made in the image and likeness of a loving God. He began in the garden of Eden with Adam and Eve. It is the place of the original relationship and the original sin.

In September 1998 the Lord gave me revelation knowledge of the purpose and significance of a garden.

The garden is a place of natural beauty,
Filled with the sights, aromas, tastes and feels
Of flowers, plants and vegetation.
It appeals in a basic way to all the senses of mankind.

The garden is a place of provision,
Filled to answer the needs of mankind,
For nutritional needs are arranged in the
Balance of one's dietary requirements.

The garden is a place of healing,
Complete with the remedy for
Any illness or disease the body
Requires to be restored to health.

The garden is a place of rest,
Providing peace and quiet from
The cares of the world and its
External influences.

The garden is a place of communion
Where the still small voice of
The Lord is audible to the listening man.

The garden is a place of prayer
Where one can go to talk to the Father
Concerning the needs of mankind and oneself,
For He longs to hear your voice.

The garden is a place of work
Where man was placed there to till the land,
To work it, to take care of it,
To dress and to keep it.

The garden is a place of life from
Where the river flows to touch and refresh
All parts of the world.

The garden is a place of anointing
As the oil flows from the tree of life,
The sap, the trunk full of
The stability and strength of God.

The garden is a place of joy
Where the birds, animals and insects of the world
Come to sing their songs of celebration
And praise to the Almighty.

The garden is a place of death
When the cessation of present life is completed and
Divine transition takes place from earth to heavenly reward.
No longer held in any fear, bondage or limitations.

The garden is a place of new creations and new life.
It is here fertilization is given
And perpetuated to provide
For new growth and continue on to others.

Beloved, the garden is a place of pure delight
Where God is pleased with all that He has created.
It is a spiritual place, a secret place of God's absolute
Lovingkindness toward those who abide and trust in Him.

For further understanding read the following scriptures: Psalm 1, Psalm 91:1-16, Genesis 2:8-14, Song of Solomon 4:12-15, Isaiah 4:6, Isaiah 12:3-5, Isaiah 58:11.

Chapter 3

His Name Is Jesus

"Nor is there salvation in any other, for there is no other name under heaven given among men by which we must be saved."

Acts 4:12

As a child I stole a toy one day. I can remember it well as though it were not that long ago. I was six years old at the time. I had gone to Woolworth's, the five-and-dime store in my town, with my mother and older brother. In the store I saw a small doll I wanted. I asked my mother for it, but she said no because we could not afford it. She told me to put it back on the shelf. She watched me put it back on the shelf, but when she turned her head I took it off the shelf again and stuffed it in my pocket.

My mother did not have her driver's license at the time, so we had walked downtown from our home, which was about a mile away. On the way back, about two long blocks from home, I decided to take my new doll out of my pocket and play with it. My mother saw the doll, and immediately she was angry with me for stealing it. When she asked me if I had stolen it, I lied and said, "No, I didn't."

Right away my mother made us turn around and go back downtown to Woolworth's store. Once there she asked for the manager and told him what had happened. In the front of the store, with everyone looking, I had to apologize to the manager for stealing the doll. That day I had a very long walk home. I learned a valuable lesson about stealing. The embarrassment alone of having to apologize was painful enough, but I had that long walk home again with my mother and brother. It was a very quiet walk.

I believe this memory is still vividly clear because it symbolizes to me how important Jesus Christ is in our lives. In my twenties I realized there was a void, an emptiness and longing in my soul that could not be satisfied by anything other than establishing a love relationship with Jesus. The Bible says that in order to have salvation we must first establish a relationship with Jesus. The Bible says, "If you confess with your mouth the Lord Jesus and believe in your heart that God has raised Him from the dead, you will be saved" (Romans 10:9, NKJV). Only when we are willing to confess our sin and turn away from the ways of the world and turn toward Christ through repentance does that salvation takes place. We cannot steal, lie or cheat our way into heaven. Salvation has to be through a relationship with the person of Jesus Christ.

Jesus is the Son of God. He is the vital key to knowing the trinity personally. If one would come into the saving grace of God, it must be by accepting Jesus Christ as Lord and Savior. Jesus is the King who reigns far above every king who ever lived.

Beloved, if you do not know Jesus Christ as your Lord and Savior, you need to come to Him by giving Him your heart. He wants to establish a loving relationship with you. As you are reading this, take a minute and bow your head and sincerely say this prayer out loud. This prayer will change your life forever.

Dear Jesus,
In Your word it is written that if I confess with my mouth that Jesus is Lord and believe in my heart that You have raised Him from the dead, I shall be saved. Therefore, Father, I come to You now. I acknowledge You as God, the Creator of heaven and earth.

Heavenly Father, I confess that I am a sinner. I have sinned against You. I renounce my past life with Satan and close the door to any of his devices. I now repent (turn away) from my sins and choose to follow and obey Christ Jesus as my Lord and Savior. I ask You, Jesus Christ, to be the Lord of my life and lead me in all areas of my life.

I receive You, Lord Jesus, as my Lord and Savior with all my heart and believe You are My King and My God.

I believe Jesus Christ is the one true sacrifice for my sins.

I believe Jesus Christ was crucified on a cross as a sacrifice for the sins of the world, sins which have blinded me and separated me from You.

I believe Jesus Christ, Your Son, took upon Himself all of my sins and the sins of all mankind.

I believe, heavenly Father, You raised Jesus Christ from the dead and He is alive and well, seated at Your right hand in heaven.

Lord, fill me with Your Holy Spirit and use my life as a willing vessel. Heavenly Father, I ask that my life will glorify You.

Thank You for forgiving me of all my sin and saving me. Jesus is now my Lord, and I am a new creation. Thank You for the truth of Your Word. Now all things have become new in Jesus Christ.

Amen.

Scriptures for further study:

John 3:16	John 14:6
John 6:37	Romans 19:9,10
John 10:10b	Ephesians 2:1-10
Romans 3:23	2 Corinthians 5:17
2 Corinthians 5:19	Romans 5:8
John 16:8,9	

Chapter 4

The First Key—Intimacy with the Holy Spirit

"Now there are diversities of gifts, but the same Spirit."

1 Corinthians 12:4

Clearly miracles are occurring today. In fact, they are taking place with a greater frequency than ever before. Jesus spoke to His beloved disciple, Nathaniel, and told him not to be amazed at the miracles he had witnessed, for before he was even called to the ministry Jesus saw him standing under a fig tree. Christ then went on to tell him that greater works the disciples would do (John 14:12). "Then He saith unto him, Verily, verily, I say unto you, Hereafter ye shall see heaven open and the angels of God ascending and descending upon the Son of Man" (John 1:51). Greater in numbers are to be the miracles believers see and perform because of Jesus' ascension into heaven after three years of ministry.

So then the cry is for the Christian to become more sensitive to the importance and the function of the Holy Spirit. The emphasis is not on the gift, but on the gift-giver. The key to living a life under the influence of the power of God is a deep and committed reverence and respect for the Holy Spirit. The key to life is not a-tailor-made-to-meet-my-needs relationship with the Holy Spirit. He is to be revered and highly regarded in our communication with Him.

The person of the Holy Spirit commands a distinct presence when a believer prays. During the communication of prayer that the Holy Spirit speaks. The Spirit of God speaks to the human spirit. His voice is close, endearing, clear and warm. His voice draws you into action, as a lover woos his beloved into an embrace. He is gentle yet powerful. The Bible says that the voice of the Lord is powerful; and that His voice is full of majesty (Psalm 29:4). Many have described the Holy Spirit as "the perfect gentleman," as He does not force Himself upon you; yet He yearns for your affection, expressed in prayer. It is the delegated authority of the Holy Spirit through whom the miraculous takes place. As a gentle Spirit, He longs to be welcomed, to be made to feel at home. In an atmosphere of worship the Holy Spirit is at His most glorious. Worship is the expression of the heart-led desire of the Christian toward the triune God. It is in worship that miracles begin to flow as undaunted rivers cascading down vast mountains and running freely. Worship connects the spirit of man to the divine Spirit of God.

There is a distinct difference between the soul of man and the Spirit of God. Witchcraft works through the soul nature of man. It appeals to the natural instincts of man. The power of Christ is always stronger than the power of Satan. In the example in Exodus 7:8-10, Moses' staff was stronger than that of Pharaoh's magicians. The staff became a snake, and Moses' snake completely devoured

Pharaoh's. God demonstrated His all-encompassing divine ability to empower His children for any encounter, as truth always destroys perversion.

During one of my early encounters with the Holy Spirit He gave me a vision one day as I was driving my car. While en route to my destination I was singing in worship; all of a sudden I saw a vision of glass vases on shelves in arrangements. The vases were made of glass in different shapes and colors. Some were round, some oblong, some tall and some short. I could see that many had dust on them while others did not. None of them had tops, and they all appeared to be empty. I asked the Lord what it meant, and He explained to me that the vases represented the different gifts which have been granted to the body of Christ. Many of the believers the vases represented were not even aware they had certain gifts. There they sat on the shelf of inactivity, day after day, month after month, year after year, often marking the pattern of their entire life.

Then I saw a great hand from heaven pour from a large vessel a hot liquid solution onto the vessels on each shelf, and they were all immediately shining clean and bright. I sensed in my spirit that the Lord was showing me what was to take place among the saints. There would be a great outpouring of the presence of the Holy Spirit; and as His Spirit increased He would cleanse many of their impurities, and vast numbers of believers would begin to operate in the gifts of His Spirit. The vision left me with a sense of peace and awe of the supernatural abilities of God. I later became familiar with the scripture that reads: "But in a great house there are not only vessels of gold and silver, but also of wood and clay, some for honor and some for dishonor. Therefore if anyone cleanses himself from the latter, he will be a vessel for honor, sanctified and useful for the Master, prepared for every good work" (2 Timothy 2:20-21).

I have seen over the years how the Holy Spirit will show Himself in various worship settings. At times He loves the melodious cacophony of sounds in praise, and at other times His desire is for the sweet, quiet stillness of worship. In fact, worship is defined as "to make obeisance, do reverence to" from *pros*, "toward," and *kuneo*, "to kiss."[13] Worship is as the welcoming of a loved one into one's embrace and the giving of one to another in a pure, undefiled manner. True, pure worship cleanses and refreshes the believer. It is the process in which the presence (anointing) of a holy, unblemished God indwells a believer and does the act of cleansing. True worship transcends far beyond man's ability and taps directly into God's supernatural ability to do what constrains human ability. One comes to understand that the essence of Christianity is not in the external act of worship; rather it is the believer becoming a worshipper. Worship is transformational. Worship becomes who one is, not simply the act of what one does.

Chapter 5

God's Design for Miracles

"God chooses the foolish things of this world to confound the wise."

1 Corinthians 1:27a

A miracle is a display of something not often seen or viewed in one's daily life. Its meaning is "a marvel or supernatural event". It is an inherent power or ability from whom the source originates beyond the natural. A miracle defies all natural law because its origins are from a supernatural God. He is the beginning of all things, and His kingdom is the place from which the source of both the natural and supernatural come. A miracle emanates directly from the throne room of God as He ushers in the genesis of existence. Whether from our individual thoughts and desires, from metaphysics to biogenetics, all of mankind's thoughts, deeds and actions are known by an omniscient Creator. Here is no measure of time, no concept of limits; and yet within there is the creation of time and limits. Such a dichotomy points to the eternal nature of God. The King is thereby always greater than His creation. This supernatural order, which far exceeds man's finite being, is only achievable through divine orchestration. The means through which our Creator can choose to display this power can vary, as it can occur through the vessel of a man or through a sovereign act of God.

Such was the case in the early 1900s. In an unknown and obscure location in California known as Azusa Street, one of the greatest events in history unfolded. It occurred in an abandoned building with an emancipated slave. William J. Seymour was born in the cornfields of southern Louisiana, with one eye visually impaired. Yet it is clear that what he lacked in physical sight was more than exceeded in spiritual sight, for he possessed an unblemished clarity to hear from the Holy Spirit. "Daddy" Seymour's nontraditional style of servant leadership drew much attention. It has been stated that he would put his head into two empty shoeboxes to pray for hours on end. This practice drew the presence of God and the attention of man.

The revival at Azusa exploded during a time of great moral depravity. Black and white slave trade, increase in alcoholism, homelessness and untreatable diseases were rampant. Human hearts proved hungry for divine intervention. It was also a time of great expectancy for something fresh and new. The Azusa miracles attracted people from all walks of life; all ethnic and socioeconomic groups were impacted. This time in history proved to be one in which the charismatic gifts manifested in greater operation. The miraculous occurred with great frequency, people were healed of sicknesses and diseases, and many received the baptism of the Holy Spirit.

The passion of Azusa took place once again in 2006 when believers from all over the world celebrated the one hundredth anniversary on the West Coast. Messages of miracles and salvation were the hallmark of the week as it was bathed in prayer and preparation months prior to the event.

One day I was lying awake in my bed with my eyes open, having read in the Bible about angelic hosts in heaven. I had just asked the Lord to show me an angel in its pure form as I wanted Him to reveal more of His personhood to me. Suddenly I saw a brilliant flash of light that went from one corner of the ceiling to the other. It appeared bright as lightning; yet it was in the shape of a face and had what appeared to be a crown on its head. I could not distinguish whether it was male or female. When it touched the opposite corner it disappeared. It took place so quickly that if I had blinked I would have missed it.

I sensed immediately that God had sent me an angel in its pure form to experience a miracle. I was so overjoyed and praised God for His beauty and His majesty.

A miracle can take place in other ways. One is in the changed health of an individual or by divine healing. Jesus healed the woman with an issue of blood (Matthew 9:20). She reached out in determination and touched Christ with more faith than others around Him as He passed by her in the crowd. The atmosphere was charged with excitement. It was explosive with people expecting to see Jesus do something special, for they knew He had done it before; and so they expected Him to do it again. The account goes on to describe how she touched the fringe of the garment Jesus wore.

Immediately Jesus felt virtue or power go out of Him, and the woman was instantly healed. No physicians were present; no unusual feat was performed; yet in a split moment in time all that woman had endured for twelve difficult years was forever removed, and her health and sense of wholeness were restored.

Often we struggle with issues in our lives that keep us from experiencing the peace of God. It could be anything from an unforgiving heart, a mindset of anger, depression, drug abuse, sexual abuse, lying, prostitution or numerous other sins. The good news is that we can find total healing when we go to God and touch Him with the hand of faith. This woman exercised faith, and Jesus did not disappoint her. She received total healing and restoration for all of the years lost by sickness. A miracle had taken place.

If you have experienced a prolonged period of pain and suffering in your physical body or wrestled with an issue of any kind that seems irresolvable, take this moment to pray this prayer:

Dear Jesus,

You know my struggles and my issues over the years. I give You each and every one, for Your Word says I can cast all my cares and anxieties on You because You care for me. Forgive me for not believing Your Word and trusting You with my life.

Thank You for setting me free from everything that has kept me in bondage. Thank You for restoring the years the locust has eaten and kept me from prospering in every area of my life. You are a mighty deliverer, and I am so grateful for Your love. Now use my life as a living testimony of Your grace and goodness to the rest of the world. Praise the name of the Lord!

Amen.

Another miracle occurred through the evidence of a changed life, such as the demon-possessed man in the synagogue (Luke 4:33-35). The Scriptures describe how the demon knew of Christ's deity, for the demons cried out that Christ had come to destroy them. Jesus Christ simply spoke a word of rebuke and commanded the demon to come out of the man. That day liberty came to the man and to his household.

I received a phone call one day that a co-worker of mine had suddenly taken ill. She was someone I knew informally, and we had shared general information from time to time, as we worked in the hospital on the evening shift together. Her daughter called and asked me to pray for her.

I was told she was fine during the evening at work. Her daughter was called to check on her when she did not show up at work the next day. When she went to the house her mother was lying unconscious in her bed with an empty cup next to the bed. She was rushed to the hospital and placed in the intensive care unit on life support. The next day her daughter called me for prayer.

I began to pray for her and placed her on my prayer list. Then the Holy Spirit gave me an unusual directive regarding this woman. The Holy Spirit kept bringing her face before me and telling me to go see her in the hospital.

Within the week I called her daughter and asked her to meet me at the hospital. She took me to the unit to see her mother. When I entered the room, the Lord showed me a vision of this woman getting out of the bed and going out of the hospital. I immediately told her daughter what God had showed me. God was not finished; I then told her I needed to go to the woman's home to see where her daughter found her. Understand this is not something I would normally do. Beyond a shadow of a doubt I knew God was directing me in this miracle.

In the woman's home I saw a cup next to her bed. God revealed to me what had happened to her. She had ingested some poison in that cup, which caused unconsciousness. I told her daughter what had happened, and she confirmed she did not know what was in the cup; but she believed something had happened to her.

God is a God of miracles. Within a few days of our visit her daughter called to tell me God sent a miracle. Her mother regained consciousness on the life support; it was removed, and finally her condition progressively improved. Within a week of her hospitalization she went home totally healed! Once again God had demonstrated His divine righteousness and mercy before us.

Jesus left for us numerous examples of wonderful miracles. Some were given to individuals while others were given to groups of people. In another example Christ showed how He gave divine provision to the multitudes (Luke 9:12-17). The people had come to hear Jesus teach the Word. Knowing they were hungry physically as well as spiritually, He fed five thousand men, not including women and children. The Scripture states that as He blessed the food, broke it and gave it there was enough food to meet the needs of the people present—with twelve full baskets left over. These actions depicted what Christ's birth, crucifixion and resurrection accomplished for the believer. Think of it—this was a creative miracle in which some material was taken and abundantly multiplied to meet the needs of many people.

These experiences were miracles because they defied all natural law and could not be explained through human sciences. Universal laws are altered when a miracle takes place. I have had times of financial lack in my life when I did not know how a bill was going to be paid or if there would be enough money for food. Then an unexpected check would arrive in the mail or a gift certificate for food. We have even had a time when we literally did not know where our next meal would come from, and with a knock at our door a neighbor sent bags of groceries. Not only would these gifts come unexpectedly, but they would also be more than enough to meet the need. I believe that because my husband and I have tithed and given offerings from our income over the years these miracles have come. These are rich examples of God's ability to give in abundance.

Early in our marriage my husband and I struggled in the area of having reliable automobiles to drive over the years. But just when we were down to the wire in needing transportation God showed up, and the cars would be fixed or the price of repair would be reduced. God's favor was being demonstrated.

We saw others abundantly blessed in having beautiful homes to live in, and yet we struggled many years to buy a decent home.

We moved frequently from place to place, having to begin again to become established in an area. So when we were finally able to purchase our first home we were once again reminded of His love and great provision in His promises toward us.

Yet we must be clear about the nature and character of God. God is not a genie in a bottle or a magician conjuring up tricks. He is the sovereign Creator of the universe who spoke the world into existence.

God has purpose, order and timing. Although He gives purpose to mankind, it is within the realm of His order and takes place in His divine timing.

Another important aspect of the miraculous is that it is not obtained by means of man's ability. We learned that nothing we did or did not do could merit the favor of God. It is freely given by virtue of the covenant relationship we have with Him. So for the skeptic who thinks the miraculous can be manipulated or duplicated, it cannot be. The manifestation of a thing can be orchestrated, but the source of its origin cannot be denied, and therein lies its unsurpassable beauty and power.

Time after time throughout the Old and New Testament shining examples of supernatural occurrences take place. In 2 Kings 6:1-7 Elisha the prophet of God raises an axe head made of iron and wood out of the water.

> Now the sons of the prophets said to Elisha, "Behold now the place before you where we are living is too limited for us. Please let us go down to the Jordan and each of us

take from there a beam and let us make a place there for ourselves where we may live." So he said, "Go." Then one said, "Please be willing to go with your servants." And he answered, "I shall go." So he went with them: and when they came to the Jordan, they cut down trees. But as one was felling a beam, the axe head fell into the water; and he cried out and said, "Alas, my master! For it was borrowed." Then the man of God said, "Where did it fall?" And when he showed him the place, he cut off a stick and threw it in there and made the iron float. And he said, "Take it up for yourself." So he put out his hand and took it.

2 Kings 6:1-7

Here Elisha, the prophet of God, used a wooden stick (part of a tree) and threw it into the water, and in so doing he located the exact spot in which the axe had sunk. The axe head rose out of the water. This is a clear example of an obvious reversal of two universal laws—the law of gravity and the law of inertia. Under natural conditions it is impossible for a stick to cause an axe to be raised out of water without a force being exerted upon it stronger than itself. In this text all natural and existing laws were bypassed to achieve an outstanding end result.

The lesson for the Christian is powerful: When the Word of God enters any situation changes occur, and miracles take place. The most wonderful example is that of salvation. When a sinner gives his life to Christ and recognizes Him as his Savior and Lord, it impacts the life of that individual for eternity. That is a miracle!

My born-again experience occurred in a hospital. I was working one night as a nurse in the newborn nursery when I began to share a dream I'd had with a co-worker in the nursery. I knew something was different about this woman. She spoke about Jesus as if she personally knew Him, and she had a joy about her that I did not understand. I later discovered she was a born-again Christian. As I began to share the dream I had experienced, she asked me if I had a personal relationship with Jesus Christ. Although I attended church it was a traditional church, and I had never heard the gospel shared in such a manner. My first response was a defensive one; I replied that I was a good person and had attended church most of my life. She quickly assured me the question she asked was about a personal, one-to-one connection with the living Jesus. I then began to listen closely to what she shared as she led me in the prayer of salvation. That night seemed long, for standing between infants who had just been born physically I gave my life to Jesus Christ.

As a newborn babe in Christ, I marveled at God's sense of timing more and more, for it took place in the same hospital where I had been physically born thirty-one years before. Over the process of time God has instructed me in the goodness of co-laboring with Him in life. He has required that I mature in my walk of faith in Him, and in it all God shows Himself to be faithful.

In the account written by the prophet Ezekiel, life is called into lifeless entities (Ezekiel 37:1-10). Here God nullifies all human reason and logic by taking the bones of dead men and causing the cycle of death and life to be reversed. In the book of Ezekiel the dry bones represent those things in one's life which are dead and ineffective; dead hopes, dead dreams and dead visions, without a prospect for the future. Bones signify the framework of the human body. So it is in the heart of God for life to come back into unmet goals and dreams to be realized. The lives and accomplishments of human beings are framed and fashioned by the vision in their heart. Many live unfulfilled lives of existence, simply going from one day to the next never reaching for something greater than they are.

Could it be that God's desire is to have new life with fresh beginnings to come into existence so that dreams and visions can live again unhindered by the past? The writing of this book took many years to accomplish, not because of its complexity, rather because of the reality of the content. God will use His time schedule in training those He has called to ministry. His school of the Holy Spirit will always include the patterns and rhythms of life. It has been that way in composing this writing while experientially living out many of the components written within these pages.

Ezekiel is an example of an instrument of God's divine grace. This Old Testament prophet yielded his life to the creative life-giving force of God to flow through him.

> Then he brought me back to the door of the temple; and there was water, flowing from under the threshold of the temple toward the east, for the front of the temple faced east; the water was flowing from under the right side of the temple, south of the altar. He brought me out by way of the north gate and led me around on the outside to the outer

gateway that faces east; and there was water, running out on the right side.

And when the man went out to the east with the line in his hand, he measured one thousand cubits, and he brought me through the waters; the water came up to my ankles. Again he measured one thousand and brought me through the waters; the water came up to my knees. Again he measured one thousand and brought me through; the water came up to my waist. Again he measured one thousand, and it was a river that could not be crossed. He said to me, "Son of man, have you seen this?" Then he brought me and returned me to the bank of the river.

Ezekiel 47:1-6

Ezekiel 47 points out the vision of the holy waters flowing from the sanctuary. This life-giving force is like the movement of water. It can be a trickling stream or a torrential flood.

I had the opportunity to travel to the Grand Canyon in Arizona. As I sat and filled my eyes with the immensely vast beauty of heaven's creation, I was fascinated with the river that lies at the base of the canyon. The river was beautiful to see as this muddy, flowing body of water, winding its way around the stony formations of the canyon, was a powerful testimony of the awesomeness of God. It reminded me of how the prophet Ezekiel spoke of the cleansing and healing abilities of the river. So it is today. It is in these unique manifestations of the Holy Spirit's presence that miracles take place.

Someone has said miracles are all around, that we see them every day. Yet the truth as evidenced by the Word is that we have not yet come to the time of the multitude of the miraculous. That is the place in history where miracles will be an everyday occurrence as when Jesus walked the earth. That time will come, as it did in the early church, when anointed vessels of God will walk into a place and from their presence healings and deliverances will spring forth in people. The Word of God runs swiftly (Psalm 147:15) to accomplish what the heart of God desires to do. Peter and John are an example in the book of Acts of how God used them to heal a man who had been lame from birth. In this miracle the two apostles gave the man what he really needed, the ability to walk on his own (Acts 3:1-10). The man "left walking, leaping and praising God" for the miracle he had received.

It has happened to others, like Katherine Kuhlman, a wonderful healing evangelist, whom God used mightily. In her book *Daughter of Destiny* she writes that God used her life so skillfully it was as if a set of 0.12mm forceps with fine, perfectly aligned teeth were grasping whatever He wanted her to grasp at the time and holding the tissue in place so the Great Physician could do the stitching and healing. Thousands upon thousands were healed as a result of her ministry. There are even documented instances of when she entered a room and the glory of the Lord was so strong upon her life that individuals would fall prostrate to the floor. Not bowing to her, but bowing in the presence of God. She was the vessel God had chosen to use for that time.

The amazing thing about Kathryn Kuhlman was that she would always recognize that the honor and praise were to the Lord and never to her. Perhaps her single greatest request during the worship services was that the people not do anything during the worship service that would grieve the presence of the Holy Spirit. For her greatest desire was that He would bless them with the fullness of His presence as evidenced by miraculous healings.

As we approach the time of Christ's second coming, the Lord will raise up a standard against Satan. The Lord will bring hope where there is no hope, peace where there is no peace and restoring health where sickness exists. Demonstrations of the miraculous works of the Holy Spirit are the way in which He will accomplish His perfect will.

Chapter 6

The Second Key— the Prophetic Vessel

"And the vessel that he made of clay was marred in the hand of the potter: so he made it again into another vessel, as it seemed good to the potter to make."

Jeremiah 18:4

The condition of the one God chooses to use in the operation of the gifts is important. It must be clearly understood that God can use any one of His children because He has all ability. Throughout the Scripture God chooses ordinary men and women He has prepared to use in this manner. One's lifelong experiences prove to be the "best university of higher learning" with the Holy Spirit Himself as the master professor.

I was sexually abused by a family member as a child, and it took many years for me to establish trust with people. My relationships would go only so far in the area of trust and transparency. Yet when I became a Christian and filled with the Holy Spirit, the distrust changed forever. I began to understand with clarity my divine rights as a child of God. This area of spiritual development did not come overnight. It took many years of seeking God and simply taking Him at His word regardless of the circumstances. In my quiet time with Him, He has told me time and time again about His love for me. A constant diet of the Word, His divine voice and a daily meal of prayer changed the negative attitude and replaced it with the God-given ability to forgive myself and others.

The Bible's example illustrates that character qualities of the vessel are important. One after another we see examples of imperfect people being used to achieve the perfect will of God. These individuals are yielded to the guidance of the Holy Spirit to make them into the vessel of honor He desires to use. A vessel is defined as a container in which something is placed. The vessel has an opening through which a substance can be placed in or poured out. People are containers of God's divine presence. Through the call of the Lord upon one's life, a believer becomes a vessel for the glory of the Lord to shine through to a darkened world. Prophets are men and women who are vessels of God's Word. They are not God or angelic beings; they are human beings who are yielded to the will of God in their lives to speak or act on behalf of God. It is the power of the Word, not the power of the vessel that transforms situations.

According to T.L. Lowery in *Apostles and Prophets—Reclaiming the Biblical Gifts,* several major terms are associated with the prophet. The Hebrew term *roeh* means "to see," while the second word *prophet* means "to speak forth" (Hebrew). The Lord uses different modes to deliver His revelatory wisdom and knowledge to the prophet. These include dreams, visions, commands, discussions and visitations. These manifestations of revelatory wisdom are how God systematically communicates with those called to the office of the prophet.

Vine's expository dictionary provides more information in two definitions for prophet. It states *prophetes* (Greek *pro* means "for" and *phemi* means "to speak") is one who "speaks forth or openly, a proclaimer of a divine message." The office of the prophet is a governmental office ordained by God given in Ephesians 4:11.

The second meaning of the prophet is *pseudoprophetes,* which means a false prophet. This is found in the Old and New Testament Scriptures in Jeremiah 14:14, and Jeremiah 23:30-32; Luke 6:26, Revelation 16:13 and 19:20. False prophets speak against the truth of God. People must watch to avoid the artificial word given by the false prophet. This was the case in Acts 13:6 when the false prophet, Barjesus, who withstood the apostles until Paul told him that he was an enemy of righteousness who goal was to pervert the ways of the Lord, and immediately the judgement and vengeance of God came upon Barjesus. The divine act of God caused the deputy who witnessed the account to acknowledge the power of God, and he believed.

Contemporary prophets listed in the New Testament are Agabus (Acts 11:27-28) and Phillip's four daughters (Acts 21:8-9). These are examples of prophetic vessels who God used to deliver divine messages to the people of Israel at strategic times in the cultures existence. In the book of Isaiah it states that the anointed one, Jesus Christ, gave power for the purpose of preaching good tidings to the poor, healing the brokenhearted, proclaiming liberty to the captives and opening the prison to those who are bound (Isaiah 61:1). The individual is the vessel God uses to remove those things which hinder the liberty of a people and of a nation.

Dr. Bill Hamon, in his book *Prophets and the Prophetic Movement,* cites that one does not have to have one of the ascension gifts of apostle, prophet, evangelist, pastor or teacher to prophesy. In fact, believers are called to be prophetic saints. These are believers who have received more training, motivation and activation enabling them to operate properly in their Holy Spirit given gifts. The believer is commissioned to live his life in a Christ-like character, the agape-like lifestyle Jesus displayed while He was on earth. It is out of this foundation that the gifts of the Holy Spirit take place through the life of the believer

Various character traits of the vessel should exist in order for the miracles to flow freely in the life of a believer. It must, however, be understood that no one is sinless or perfect with the exception of Christ. It was for that reason Jesus came. His purpose was to redeem imperfect mankind into a full relationship with a perfect God. To accomplish that task He had to come both as deity and as humanity. He had to come to earth fully empowered to achieve the purpose for which He existed. Christ came as the only flawless example for sinful man to follow.

Repentance is the beginning point of mankind as the believer develops in the gifts of the Spirit. To repent is to turn away from sin. Numerous times in the Old Testament Scripture we read that Israel committed sin by embracing the foreign gods of other cultures and their lifestyles. God repeatedly admonished them to repent. When this took place the Jewish people would once again be restored so they could experience the divine favor of God. His desire is for the whole of man, and in turning to Him God promised to make Israel a wall of bronze (signifying a strong protective structure).

In reviewing some of His character traits seven aspects appear to be important. First, the individual must be willing to be used. *Willingness* means a readiness, desirous and prompt. Psalm 40:8 says, "I delight to do thy will, O my God." The vessel used by God is yielded. Great pleasures come into one's heart from a willingness to obey the Holy Spirit. The individual's outstanding desire needs to be to see God's plan take place, and so he is available for the Holy Spirit. The more willing the person is to hear clearly from the Holy Spirit, the more wholly and effectively the Spirit of God can use him. God called David a man after His own heart because David was willing to follow God fully. David obeyed God when he went into battle against Goliath and later became king over all of Israel (1 Samuel 17:50 and 1 Chronicles 11:1-3).

The believer's willingness to be used by God will enhance the release of the power of God. This release can take place through song or word during corporate worship. This aspect of the character of the vessel pertains to what God is doing in the earth and thus brings a fresh inspired word from the heart of God. A willing heart holds faithfulness close to it because it recognizes it is our Lord who is faithful and steadfast in His love toward us in everything. God desires that we co-labor with Him willingly.

In my years of ministry, as I struggled with personal insecurities, I often had a "yes, Lord" of confirmation with my mouth yet did not have a "yes, Lord" in my actions. I learned that when the Scripture says to let your "yes be yes" and your "no be no," it is indeed serious business. Understand that God is a God of grace and goodness; but for those who desire to dwell and exist in the secret place of His glory the spoken word is of the utmost importance. God wants mature sons and daughters, and so often through life experiences He develops mature and responsible children. Throughout Scripture God has shown that differences such as gender, race and socio-economic backgrounds do not limit Him. All He wants is a vessel to whom and through whom He can demonstrate His goodness, righteousness and grace.

Another aspect of the vessel is that an individual must be consecrated or set apart, as one devoted to God. In Exodus 28:3-4 Aaron was consecrated to the office of a priest. This took place during an elaborate ceremony in which the Levites responsible for the making of the garments were given divine insight and wisdom to design the garments worn. The clothes Aaron wore as well as the ceremony signified to the people that a distinction had occurred. It was a holy thing unto the Lord. The office of the high priest was given to demonstrate God's order and glory to Israel.

The Lord consecrates vessels to display to the world His honor and majesty. One becomes fashioned into Christ's image when called to live a holy life. His presence permeates every area of our lives. Nothing is hidden and nothing is left unchanged by the power of God. Every sin and every thought are open before Him, and yet He loves us unconditionally. The knowledge of this truth is too awesome to comprehend fully. It is because of His great love that we stand forgiven, cleansed and made whole. He clothes us with His righteousness, bathes us with His glory and surrounds us with His marvelous grace.

In 2 Kings 4:3 we read, "Then he said, 'Go borrow the vessels abroad of all thy neighbor's, even *empty* vessels, borrow many." Through her obedience to the prophet's instructions the woman received a blessing. She was told to gather empty containers, go into her home and close her door. Once inside she was to pour oil into the containers. The woman began with only a little oil. Miraculously the empty vessels became the holders of precious oil. It was the oil she desperately needed to live on. There was more than enough for her and her son to live on. So it is when a person allows the Lord to empty us of our wants and desires in life. God can fill us with the presence of the Holy Spirit and provide more than enough for us. The vessel must be empty of its own agenda and open to instruction as the Holy Spirit brings clarity. It is when we open ourselves to more of the power and glory of God that He alone fills the empty places in our lives with His divine presence.

Intercessory prayer becomes the catalyst for the vessel to be filled. I learned that as a Christian I am called to live a life of prayer. My position is not simply to pray for my needs or the needs of my loved ones, but to pray for the world. When the door is closed to distraction, destruction and unbelief, circumstances change, and the miraculous works of God take place. Areas of lack become prosperous.

I can remember one Christmas when we were struggling financially. I had been praying and crying out to God for a change in the situation we faced. After paying bills and getting food, we had no more money for gifts, and decorations were few. One evening as I stepped out of my car and looked down I discovered a twenty dollar bill, enough for a Christmas tree. The next day I received a check in the mail; it was enough for gifts and decorations, and I had some money left over. It was a glorious Christmas. God filled my vessel with faith and the knowledge of Him who provides for us.

Purity is the condition of the heart of one who is genuine about being undefiled by sin. In Titus 1:15 we read that "to the pure all things are pure" Christians are called to be pure before God in all their actions. No hidden motives or agendas are to exist in the life of the believer. It is not to say that one cannot have things that are secret in a righteous sense; yet it is to distinguish that no sin is to have a place in the life of the Christian. Purity of the heart comes when one's actions stem from undefiled motives When a vessel is pure, everything reflected in its life is to be pure. There exists a transparency in the life of the believer. It is only through the finished work of Christ on the cross of Calvary that allows a believer to live a life of purity. When a vessel is pure, more light can be reflected through it, such as a light bulb reflecting the brilliance of the electrical source to which it is connected. Spots on the bulb hinder its ability to reflect clarity of light.

As Christians we are called to be both salt and light shining forth the brilliance of Christ's love to the world around us. It is the work of the Holy Spirit, who takes great care for us as He works out any impurities within us to produce an unrestrained and undefiled vessel, bringing one to a degree of purity and cleansing unmatched by human attempts or ability. For years I tried on my own to live a perfect life, always appearing as though everything was in order and under my control, until I came to understand that what I so longed for only God could complete in me. So when I began to be serious about "letting go and letting God," I saw changes take place in my personality and in the impact I had on others. I recognized that to strive to be flawless was legalism, and it was impossible. God only requires that I seek Him in righteousness, and He does the rest.

Psalm 126:6 declares, "He who goes to and fro weeping carrying his bag of seed shall *doubtless* come again with a shout of joy, bringing his sheaves with him." The Lord is mighty in power. It is He who turns negative circumstances around. It is He who tills our hearts with pure joy causing all doubts to leave. For the one who has shed precious tears and cried to the Lord, the Lord turns each delicate heartfelt tear into bouquets of joy.

My life was a mess. I used to be scared of everything. I was afraid of people, afraid of being myself and afraid of enjoying life until I began to understand the importance of praise in the life of the believer. The door had been opened for fear to enter my life as a result of the sexual abuse when I was a young girl.

After I became saved I was completely healed of all my fears through praise. I began to understand the various characteristics of God. One such aspect is His sense of humor. When I see my life more through the eyes of faith it takes on a whole new meaning. I was the second of three children, and my parents named me Judith. It was a name I used to dislike since my siblings often teased me when we were young because of my name. One day I read that my name in Hebrew means "praise." In fact, Herbert Lockyer writes in his work *All the Women of the Bible* that Judith is "a pure Hebrew name which is the feminine form of Jehudie," a proper name with the same sense of Judah, "praise." In Jewish history there is the apocryphal book which bears the name of Judith. In that book Judith was a heroine who was known for brilliantly and courageously saving her people from their attackers.

Now do not misunderstand. I have come to understand my value in light of the grace of God in my life. It is God's grace that enables me to accomplish His will for my life without my having to be or act perfect. Yet I had to first discover who He created me to be. Beloved, once you come to Christ, He wants you to know who He created you to be. You are not a copy of someone else; you are a distinctly and uniquely created and divinely designed individual. I found this out for myself when I realized the significance of praise and worship to God in everything in my life. Praise cleared my heart and mind of all the clutter that had set up shop there. Whenever I worship and praise God, His presence clears my mind and transforms me more and more into His wonderful image (Romans 12:1-2). Each of us must discover who we are in Christ.

One day I found the truth in understanding the significance of the worship experience during the harvest time for the Hebrew nation in the Old Testament. A blast of a mighty trumpet called a shofar and a shout of joy signaled that the time of celebration was at hand. It marked a confidence and a certainty that came when the food of the harvest was ripe and ready for reaping. The shout was raised because it was an expression of the bounty and richness of the crop. For the one who loves the Lord, boldness comes to the heart alleviating all doubts and all fears. "Beloved I wish above all things that you might prosper and be in health, even as your soul prospers" (1 John 2:3). The truth is that the victory of all doubts and all fears has already been won and all that needs to be done is to receive it by faith. This brings bountiful joy and peace.

A *yielded* vessel is one that produces. Leviticus 26:3-4 states, "If you walk in My statutes and keep My commandments, and perform them, then I will give you rain in its season; the land shall yield its produce, and the trees of the field shall yield their fruit" A yielded vessel is a person who produces for the kingdom of heaven. God can use this vessel to see miracles happen, for others to receive salvation and for answers to prayer to come to pass in an instant of time. This person must be obedient to hear the voice of the Lord and to follow it. Obedience comes quickly and without hesitation or restraint, yielding an end result which richly glorifies God.

Anointed means to rub or smear with oil as in consecrating. Exodus 30:30 reads, "And you shall anoint Aaron and his sons and consecrate them that they may minister as priests to me." The Lord was very explicit to Israel regarding the anointing. In Exodus 30:31 He says, "And you shall speak to the sons of Israel saying this shall be holy anointing oil to me throughout your generations." The presence of the Holy Spirit is a precious anointing upon the believer. His presence is what makes the difference in a vessel that is used in the working of miracles and one that is not. The process of rubbing or smearing oil over the priests was to ensure that the oil would saturate the priests thoroughly. The oil could be seen with its glistening qualities and smelled with its sweet aroma, for it was made of the finest and choicest spices of the land. The end result was the distinction of holiness.

From the first time the priests were placed in office the impact upon the people was tremendous because they knew the priests were to function as the mediators between the presence of an undefiled God and His beloved creation. The people of Israel knew that with God on their side mighty would be the deeds they would accomplish and many would be the victories won. All this was because of the anointing. Each believer now has access to the anointing, breaking every yoke of bondage, because of the finished work of Jesus. There is no longer the need for a human mediator. Each of us can go directly to Jesus in prayer, but we must follow His pattern to receive His blessing.

Chapter 7

Understanding the Process

"For no other foundation can anyone lay than that which is laid, which is Jesus Christ."

1 Corinthians 3:11

The realm of the miraculous needs to be a place where the believer desires to lives daily. How pointless it is to see the beauty of the miraculous and not be drawn to the richness of its source. One area of error is to forget that the purpose of the supernatural is to show the living power and majesty of our Father God to mankind. The message must not be to run to the gift store for the gift, but rather to run to one's heavenly Father, who is the giver of the gift. God's Word says we must seek first the kingdom of God and His righteousness (Matthew 6:33).

The greatest miracle of all is salvation. It is knowing you are eternally secure in the mighty hand of God. Salvation gives one an overwhelming sense of the greatness and vast tapestry of God's unmerited love. Miracles thrive where salvation exists. There is the creation of an atmosphere filled with expectation and excitement.

The bride eagerly awaits the bridegroom, with pure and utter delight in the union, as with the sovereign and graceful Father who liberally gives to His children.

Another point of importance is to recognize that the nature of mankind is to analyze and rationalize. The Bible clearly states that we must not be wise in our own eyes (Proverbs 3:7). Instead we must avoid the temptation to rationalize the work of God. An illustration would be that as the gift of healing is taking place, one may ask why everyone is not healed. How easy it is to explain it away as some secret sin or an individual's lack of faith. What a rank odor that must send to the nostrils of God. Instead we must recognize the Lord's divine sovereignty and His total ability to release His miraculous. The essential truth is that God loves us with a love our finite minds cannot fully comprehend. In moments when we sense His powerful love, He pours on us liberally, we come to the reality that His love is without limits. How frail we as human beings are before our loving heavenly Father.

In the Old Testament a nation would come to a decision over questions by casting lots before the people (Joel 3:3). God is calling His people in this time to make a decision for seeking His presence. The ultimate reason for which we are created is to worship God. In mankind's search for meaning it is the spirit of man which longs for fulfillment. It is not until a person gives his or her life to Christ and accepts Him as the Savior who brings salvation and the Lord who destines a life that time and complete satisfaction take place. Your desire in life must be to live life as a part of God's glorious family, part of His redemptive plan. Your desire must be as a vessel through which miracles can flow.

Miracles are as unique as God who creates them. God has fashioned each person who has ever lived to be a separate entity, uniquely different. He has designed miracles for His glory. The miracles bring into focus the reality of the living God. The life we live is always changing as each day is fresh and new. As seasons change and people change, so the miraculous power of the Holy Spirit is fluid and changes with the current of God's design and plan. A river runs from point A to point B, touching various areas along the way. Everything that is touched by the river of life flows with life and is healed (Ezekiel 47:9). Sickness and disease are healed. Emotional wounds are made whole. Spiritual soundness takes place—all in this healing place where the waters of the Holy Spirit flow. We must rest assured that miracles are God's proven way of affirming to mankind that He is still in control. It is a way of life, the place of liberty, joy and peace. It is the place where the Christian should long to be.

The believer who wants to walk in the blessings of Christianity must live a life of prayer and holiness. It is in the directly orchestrated communication between God and man that all fears, doubts and anxieties melt away. These issues are replaced with the confidence, boldness and power of an awe-inspiring Father. God lives in miracles, and we should desire His divine presence through the miraculous.

I had received word that my only brother, John, was terminally ill. We watched as this once young and vibrant man struggled with a terminal illness. He went from being robust and energetic to a debilitated and frail condition. He had a love of people which was communicated once he walked into a room. Yet for most of his life he did not have a personal relationship with Christ. Finally, growing weaker by the day, he decided to accept Jesus as his personal Lord and Savoir. How exciting it was to have him say the prayer of salvation and see his life change. His change was not in a physical manifestation; his change was within the spiritual transformational power of a living God. His countenance grew gentler, and his face glistened with a heavenly vibrancy.

He died late one Friday evening in the hospital. I had been with him earlier that evening, making him comfortable and caring for his needs. As I eulogized my brother at his funeral service I was able to share with those present that he was in heaven with his Savior Jesus Christ. God is a loving and gracious Father, whose love stretches from eternity past to eternity future.

The Christian life is one of sacrifice. The sacrifice is not a physical one; rather it is a spiritual one. Christ does not require us to do what He accomplished on Calvary. It is already a finished work. Only Christ could die as a sacrifice for others. No longer is the sacrifice of bulls and goats needed. Christ is the perfect sacrifice, whose death on the cross transcends all possible barriers and limitations. Therefore the Christian is now spiritually free from all of life's challenges. It does not negate the existence of problems and issues in the believer's life; it simply means that the problems and issues are never to hold the believer captive. Because of the work of Christ the Christian can live a life of peace and joy.

Chapter 8

The Third Key—the Lifestyle of Prayer

"Therefore everyone who hears these words of mine and puts them into practice is like a wise man who built his house on the rock."

Matthew 7:24

Prayer is the communication connection with God. To pray is to address God, to supplicate or to implore Him. Prayer for the believer is the empowering ability to communicate with an all-encompassing, loving God. Prayer is vital for the believer, as it is making the right connection to God. A sincere Christian, one who is real about his or her relationship with God and about living life as a disciplined one, prays. One recognizes the seriousness in the importance of prayer. Prayer is the essence of communication with God. It is the release of God's design through a human vessel. Some have said that prayer is actually God speaking His heart to His beloved creation by the individual. It is vital to the Christian faith that the believer must pray. Jesus spent forty days in the wilderness fasting and praying; when He had completed the time praying, He was empowered in the strength of God (Mark 1:12-13, Matthew 4:1-2, Luke 4:1-2). It is the life source that links the Christian to God. Prayer is the expression of God's will through the believer, either for oneself or for others.

From my early days after becoming a Christian, I would spend extended times in prayer. I wanted more of God's presence, and I learned early that only He is able to fill the deepest voids in my heart. I came to a place, however, in which my prayers seemed shallow. I felt limited and restricted, and I was not able to hear God's direction for my life.

Early one morning as I was about to begin in prayer, kneeling at my bedside, I heard distractive sounds all around me. I heard birds singing, dogs barking and cars driving by outside my house. Despite this I prayed for a short period of time and went back to bed. Shortly afterward I was awakened from my sleep with a spiritual vision. My bed was shaking as if in an earthquake. Startled and confused, I sat straight up in bed as I heard the Lord give me Scripture from Matthew 7:26: "But everyone who hears these words of mine and does not put them into practice is like a foolish man who built his house on the sand." I immediately understood that God was speaking to me about the importance of prayer, and I fell on my face and began to intercede with a new fervency and zeal. Since that day my prayer life has never been the same.

It is impossible to develop into Christian maturity without a life of prayer. That is why Satan attempts to blind the believer so adamantly to living a lifestyle of prayer. Jesus spent forty days and forty nights in the wilderness praying and fasting to be empowered to clearly accomplish the will of God for His life (Matthew 4:1-11, Mark 1:12-45). Every believer must discipline themselves to pray daily.

Prayer has two aspects. There is the personal aspect of prayer, when the believer prays for his personal needs and wants. This is when prayer is self focused and directed. This is important to strengthen the faith of the believer in the beginning stages of the Christian lifestyle. Over the years as the child of God matures and grows it is expected that this type of prayer would develop and change in its nature and content as the believer exercises a greater demonstration of faith in God and in His Word. Most of us have heard the preacher challenge the church not to simply pray "for us four and no more." Indeed personal prayer is important because it matures us as believers as we come to know more about God. But if left to be the single focal point of one's prayer life it can become shallow and selfish.

The second type is intercessory prayer. In this prayer the believer is praying for the needs of others. This aspect of prayer focuses on service to others. The individual who is praying willingly communicates to God on behalf of the affairs of others. This prayer is vital in the Christian experience as it connects believers together in unity, under the direction of the Holy Spirit. This is the level of servitude that truly honors God's kingdom. Kingdom principles always support and favor those who willingly and cheerfully give to the needs of others. Praying for others is a form of serving. Galatians 5:13 tells us, "...only do not use liberty for an occasion to the flesh,, but by love serve one another."

Prayer carries transcending and transforming power with it. One could pray for an individual they know well or they could pray for someone they will never meet in their lifetime. Prayer is not confined to time and space, for it is the spoken word that is released into the atmosphere, changes, and promotes transformation as it accomplishes its purpose.

It is always important to begin prayer with praise and adoration to God. Praise prepares the way into the throne room of God. There are various levels of praise. Praise opens the way into the kingdom of God; yet often the believer who enters into praise is distracted by other things on an earthly plain as well. When the believer enters into high praise (known as hallelujah), a spiritual awareness has been tapped into that is a dimension of the supernatural in which miracles are birthed. Faith is the foundation for this dimension. Faith pleases God.

The believer must choose his or her words carefully. Words carry weight, and they have power and ability. As children, many of us said, "Sticks and stones may break my bones, but words will never hurt me." That is not actually true. Words can hurt. Words can damage emotions, break relationships and cause havoc in the lives of people. The Christian must be aware of evil forces such as witchcraft prayers and curses, curses from other Christians and negative proclamations spoken toward them directly or indirectly that will try to derail the will of God in their life.

Curses can be destructive and must be broken off the lives of believers. Just as we must first recognize that sin exists and that we are sinners, to break destructive habits and behaviors in our lives we must break the pattern. The breakthrough takes place by following the biblical pattern. We must acknowledge that we are in a spiritual battle, a war for the spirit and soul of mankind. It is not a physical battle we fight. It is a spiritual one for which we as believers must be spiritually armed and ready to use the unlimited power prayer has for us. The field for the battle is the unseen spiritual realm. The believer is to engage in the battle with the truth of the Scripture.

> Now I, Paul, myself am pleading with you by the meekness and gentleness of Christ—who in presence am lowly among you, but being absent am bold toward you. But I beg you that when I am present I may not be bold with that confidence by which I intend to be bold against some, who think of us as if we walked according to the flesh. For though we walk in the flesh, we do not war according to the flesh. For the weapons of our warfare are not carnal but mighty in God for pulling down strongholds, casting down arguments and every high thing that exalts itself against the knowledge of God, bringing every thought into captivity to the obedience of Christ, and being ready to punish all disobedience when your obedience is fulfilled.
>
> 2 Corinthians 10:1-6

Think of it—God promises He will handle all of our enemies when we war in the spirit. That is an exciting truth. Believers are not to be sitting ducks for the enemy to destroy at will; instead we are to be engaged in a real battle, a fight between good versus evil, right versus wrong, and truth versus lies. Truth wins when we speak the truth in love against all curses and negative deeds sent from Satan and stand strong against them by faith.

As in any military battle we are to engage in battle dressed in the right spiritual attire. In Ephesians 6:11, 14-17, we are commanded to "put on the whole armor of God, that you may be able to stand against the wiles of the devil . . .Stand therefore, having your loins girt about with truth, and having on the breastplate of righteousness; And your feet shod with the preparation of the gospel of peace; Above all, taking the shield of faith, wherewith ye shall be able to quench all the fiery darts of the wicked. And take the helmet of salvation, and the sword of the Spirit, which is the word of God. There it is. The battleground, the weapons and the armor of our warfare are stated clearly for us to use as God designed.

Right words spoken can be like "apples of gold in settings of silver" (Proverbs 25:11). The meaning is that it is something precious, to be desired. Words spoken in prayer have the ability to alter history and steer it in a positive direction.

Heavenly Father, in Christ Jesus' holy name, I thank You for Your Word in Numbers 6:24-26. Heavenly Father, I pray that You will bless us and keep us. I pray that You will make Your face shine upon us and be gracious to us. I pray that You will lift up Your countenance upon us and give us peace. Lord Jesus, thank You for Your many blessings to us.

Amen

Another example of the miraculous in prayer is how God warns the believer of trials to come. I was sound asleep one night when I was awakened by a voice. As I lay beside my husband, one word was spoken by an audible voice. This voice was unlike any voice I had ever heard before. It was all encompassing, serenely strong and powerful. The voice said only one word; yet because of this significance I was able to get the message that something very important was about to take place. The one word was "**LISTEN.**" I immediately knew it was the voice of God speaking directly to me. I responded with a "yes, Lord" and went into an extended period of prayer. God was supernaturally preparing me for something that was about to happen to me.

The next day, as I returned home, my life changed dramatically. For the next seven years, I raised my children as a single parent. During this time I discovered what it was to grow into a more intimate relationship with the Lord. God began to grow my experiences in Him daily throughout the difficulties of my life. How could I raise my children successfully to be well developed and emotionally solid individuals? Would these difficulties damage their emotional, psychological and spiritual development? Learning to listen to God was the pivotal point in all my relationships. First, I began to understand God's ways by prayer and then by the reading of the Word of God. It was with this developing sensitivity to hear from an ever-speaking God that I started to grow in my walk and successfully be led through my difficult life experiences.

Corporate Prayer

Prayer is essential in the corporate setting. Time and again the Scriptures encourage the believer not to forsake the time of coming together in unity (Psalm 133:1-3). This includes intercessory prayer. It is vital to pray together with other believers for a common cause. Prayer produces a synergy which is an unstoppable force. The Scripture says, "One can put a thousand and two can put ten thousand to flight"

(Deuteronomy 32:30). As believers follow the plan of God and walk according to His plan and purposes, miracles come to pass. Prayer brings the supernatural power of God. When a believer prays, he releases a power greater than any human-made experience or ability. It is the same power that created the universe and everything contained within it. It is the all-encompassing power of God.

At times this power is so great that it can cause the human body to shake or vibrate as God's power is released into a human vessel. In these cases, it is as though God overcharges the electrical impulses within a person's body, surging one with new strength and a fresh touch of His presence. God lives in miracles through the divine revelations He gives in prayer.

The intercessor is called to live a holy life to effectively be used by the Lord. The Scripture states that God "wondered" that there was no intercessor available and ready to pray (Isaiah 59:16). Holiness is brought about by living a disciplined lifestyle. This means that this individual does not willfully sin or live a life of impurity. Things such as unforgiveness, bitterness, anger, fear and jealousy are not practiced in the life of the intercessor. The holiness of God in the life of a believer cannot co-exist with sin. The disciplined life is one that pursues prayer.

There must also be an understanding that this individual is not expected to know it all or to have all the answers. In fact, for any human being to have all knowledge is impossible; this is God's domain. Our wisdom and the perfection for knowledge can only be found in our open, continual relationship with Jesus Christ. That is the distinct difference between the doctrine of grace and legalism. Grace merits our growth through our clear understanding of Christ living on the inside of us.

Legalism dictates that we must perform in a certain way or do certain things in order to deserve God's love. The law is given as our schoolmaster, and grace is given as our liberator (Galatians 3:24-25). The period of the Mosaic law has been fulfilled and completed with the coming of Jesus Christ. The Christian now embraces grace by faith in God and His ability to fulfill His Word. You must pray for an understanding of more of God's grace in your life by faith. The Scripture tells us, "Therefore it is of faith that it might be according to grace, so that the promise might be sure to all the seed, not only to those who are of the law, but also to those who are of the faith of Abraham, who is the father of us all" (Romans 4:16).

Corporate or collective prayer is essential for the believer to mature in the church. People must be taught the principles of prayer. It must never be taken for granted or assumed that people know how to pray or that one clearly understands the true value of prayer.

Church leadership must take the primary role and constantly teach the foundation of prayer. Prayer is the framework of Christianity, as it is by prayer that a person comes to Christ by salvation and by prayer one matures in his or her lifestyle. It is one of the most powerful forces available in existence for the believer. Prayer enables the believer to fulfill the will of God. We must pray.

Christ left us a pattern for prayer, a script by which to establish our prayers. In this prayer He completes the full spectrum of the foundation format that the disciple of Jesus Christ needs to engage in. In Luke 11 it was the disciples who upon seeing Jesus' lifestyle of prayer inquired of Him how to pray. Christ then gives this beautiful model for Christendom:

> When you pray, say:
> Our Father in heaven,
> Hallowed be Your name.
> Your kingdom come,
> Your will be done,
> On earth as it is in heaven.
> Give us day by day our daily bread.
> And forgive us our sins,
> For we also forgive everyone who is indebted to us.
> And do not lead us into temptation,
> But deliver us from the evil one.
>
> Luke 11:2-4

What a simplistically powerful admonishment from our Lord to begin our time of prayer by first looking heavenward to God who is the center. It reminds us of His holiness and sanctification and the reigning kingdom of God, with His provision and protection from the satanic enemy. In praying this prayer we are part of the kingdom of God and seek the will and actions of God's government which differs from the earthly government. God's rules, laws and mandates are clearly outlined in the sacred Scripture. In understanding this one is able to ask that the kingdom of God come and have preeminence over and above the government of man. This powerful action is what transforms men's hearts and lives and expands to impact those within the sphere of influence.

As fallible human beings we ask a perfect God to forgive us for any sin, known and unknown, which would keep us from complete relationship with Him. When this takes place the victoriously triumphant kingdom of God is manifested. Temptations will come, but the ability to overcome them is found in our awe-inspiring relationship with the Lord of lords and King of kings.

I believe that prayer in the corporate setting must establish priorities in its delivery. When believers come together to pray, it is essential that a spirit of unity take place. This is the experiential synergy that occurs when believers come together. It is this oneness that Satan detests. This is what defeats him and destroys his work. James 4:7 tells us, "Therefore submit to God. Resist the devil, and he will flee from you." First the believers must submit to God and His kingdom; then one is empowered to resist the devil, and Satan must flee. There are no options here. Satan must leave.

Prayer is vital to one's relationship with God. No relationship can exist without clear and purposeful communication between two parties. This is the pattern established by God in the book of Genesis. It is here that one can see how it was important to God to spend time and talk to Adam and Eve in the cool of the garden. It was in this complete place of provision that mankind was to spend time fellowshipping with God face to face by communication. Man was permitted to see God in the form of His glory in paradise. This is the picture of the most profoundly beautiful and limitless forms of communication which became the example for how God would relate to mankind after the birth of His Son Jesus.

Chapter 9

Dwelling in the Supernatural

"And let them make me a sanctuary that
I may dwell among them"
Exodus 25:8

God's supernatural realm is the place where one must desire to exist or live. It is not a physical place like a house or an apartment. The supernatural realm is the place of continual communion and fellowship with God. In this place the supernatural becomes the distinct expectation. It is God's desire that we put a demand or a pull on His holy presence. Mankind is of no comparison to the creative and life-giving ability of the Creator of the universe. Everything that exists was first spoken into existence by the unlimited creative ability of God.

The pattern to follow was thereby given from God to man in the Scripture. John 1:1 makes it clear: "In the beginning was the Word, and the Word was with God, and the Word was God. He was in the beginning with God. All things were made through Him, and without Him nothing was made that was made." This passage of Scripture firmly supports the deity of Jesus Christ, as He is the "Word made flesh and dwelling among us" (John 1:14). How then did Jesus "dwell" among us? What were the distinctive characteristics of His dwelling or existing among man as He walked the earth? When you study the Scriptures it is plain to see that He led a simple life, unencumbered by the cares of the world, and yet His impact was tremendously important. The pattern that is distinct is that He prayed continuously, He prayed earnestly, and He prayed the Word. I believe that the times we are living in are some of the best times as well as some of the worst times in the history of the world. As we contend for the faith and determine to live a stable Christian life, it must be determined that the stability is not found in the external source of those things around us; rather it is found in the internal transformation of the presence with a living God. It is therefore imperative that one's success in this life, either in business, politics, education or the church community, must be directly related to a strong Christian foundation. It is of the utmost importance that one lives a life of strong moral character. This is not the supernatural, but it provides an excellent base of support and strength on which it can be built and sustained and demonstrated to the world.

    I received my spiritual upbringing in a Methodist church in what seems like a long time ago. When I was later called to the ministry, God led me back to the AME Zion church of my upbringing to serve there for several years. The first sermon I preached was taken from the scriptural text 2 Corinthians 5:17. Although I was a nervous, fragile young lady at the time, once I opened up the sacred Scripture

I was empowered by God's love. I learned then that God had given me a longing and a love to preach and to teach His Word.

As a child, I set out to make a model plane with my brother. It was his plane, and he had the parts for it kept neatly in a box. As we proceeded to put the plane together, however, we noticed that the instructions were missing from the box. We searched in the box among the plastic parts and found nothing. We looked on the cover of the box and still found nothing. The instructions were missing. We began to put the parts together as best we could without any written instructions, but it took a very long time, was haphazardly done and became frustrating in the process. We fussed, as siblings often do, through the process. It seemed he didn't want to try any of my suggestions, and of course I was right.

Finally, fatigued and discouraged with what was supposed to be an enjoyable activity, we gave up making the plane. Later that evening when our father came home from work, seeing our discouragement, he promised to get us another model plane. Several days later he did just that, and this one had better parts to assemble which fit together with ease, and it even came with a set of instructions. We were excited. Putting together the plane was fun. When we finished the plane looked great and lasted for many, many years. It was well worth the wait and the work.

Just like the assembly of the plane by my brother and me, God is very practical in His dealings with us. He is not spooky and scary. Instead He is loving and kind, and He wants nothing more than to be given the opportunity to love us freely. He gave us a set of instructions we can follow, and when we do we can have the greatest joy imaginable in our lives.

He gives us a secret place to live in His divine protection and care. Psalm 91 tells us that we can exist in the secret place of the Most High. There is no one higher than God, and so there is no place in the existence of man that gives more protection. He has an overwhelming presence which gives a shadow. It is in this shadow, the shade emitted from His great limitless light, given to keep us from the toxic heat of life, that we find the shield of protection. Those who commune with God are safe with Him. The Almighty Himself is where His shadow is. The believer should confess aloud that God is their refuge and fortress. When danger comes the believer must take hold of the Word and go to the Lord for shelter and not to the arm of the flesh. In the forest when a predator comes, animals such as birds, foxes and deer flee to a place of protection and hiding. We flee too, but not to a structural place or designation. We run to the Lord in prayer. It is here that the answer to the situation occurs. Beloved, when we are secure in God, we can rejoice in all situations because we know beyond a doubt that the Greater One lives within us.

Let me encourage you, as you end this book, to open your heart to the reality that God lives in miracles and He desires to live in you. Get to know Him and love Him. He is a sovereign God. Invite Him into your environment by heartfelt praise and worship; purposely create an atmosphere for Him and then witness His miracles flow to and through you to others. You can do this by spending quality time with Him in prayer and the study of His magnificent words to you in the Scripture. Get to know His character, His ways, and His will for your life. I guarantee you that you will not be disappointed. Don't treat Him as a "jack in the box" God; He is not. He is vastly more than that. Remember He is the Creator of the universe. Love Him and entreat His presence, and your life will be blessed far beyond measure. I end this writing to you with His Word, for I believe there is nothing I can say that is more powerful than these words from the book of Ephesians. Why not memorize them and let them become a part of who you are? I have, and these words constantly bring me great peace and joy.

For this reason I bow my knees to the Father of our Lord Jesus Christ, from whom the whole family in heaven and earth is named, that He would grant you, according to the riches of His glory, to be strengthened with might through His Spirit in the inner man, that Christ may dwell in your hearts through faith, that you, being rooted and grounded in love, may be able to comprehend with all the saints what is the width and length and depth and height; to know the love of Christ which passes knowledge, that you may be filled with all the fullness of God (Ephesians 3:14-19).

Shalom

Endnotes

Chapter 1: The God of the Supernatural

[1] W.E. Vine, *Vine's Complete Expository Dictionary of Old and New Testament Words* (Nashville, TN: Thomas Nelson, 1996), 412.

[2] William M. Taylor, *The Gospel Miracles* (London: Hamilton Adams Co., 1880), 10-11.

[3] *Vine's Complete Expository Dictionary*, p. 328.

[4] Arthur Guyton, M.D., *Textbook of Medical Physiology,* 4th edition. (Philadelphia, PA: W.B. Saunders, 1971), 456-457.

[5] John Deere, *Surprised by the Power of the Spirit* (Grand Rapids, MI: Zondervan, 1993), 26.

[6] Francis Robert, *Come Away, My Beloved* (Ojai, California: King's Farspan Inc., 1970), 22.

[7] Charles Colson and Nancy Pearcey, *How Now Shall We Live?* (Carol Stream, IL: Tyndale House, 1999, xiii.

[8] Nancy Pearcey, *Total Truth* (Wheaton, IL: Crossway, 2005).

[9] James Montgomery Boice, *Foundations of the Christian Faith* (Downer's Grove, IL: InterVarsity Press, 1986), 149-153.

Chapter 2: Understanding Divine Order

[10] John D. Morris, Ph.D, "Is It Scientifically Impossible for Miracles to Occur?" ICR Internet access, http://www.icr.org/article/it-scientifically-impossible-for-miracles-occur/. [11]Boice, *Foundation of the Christian Faith*, 153-155.

Chapter 3: His Name Is Jesus

[12]Word Ministries Inc. *Prayer that Avails Much,* vol. 1. (Tulsa, OK: Harrison House, 1989), 47.

Chapter 4: The First Key—Intimacy with the Holy Spirit

[13]*Vine's Complete Expository Dictionary,* p. 686.

Chapter 5: God's Design for Miracles

[14]*Webster's New Expanded Dictionary* (Miami, FL: P.S.I. & Associates, 1991), 215.

[15]Frank Bartlman, *Azusa Street* (New Kensington, Pa: Whitaker House, 1982).

[16]Katherine Kuhlman, *Daughter of Destiny* (South Plainfield, NJ: Bridge Publishing, 1976), 190-191.

Chapter 6: The Second Key—The Prophet's Vessel

[17]*Webster's New Expanded Dictionary,* 366.

[18]T.L. Lowery, *Apostles and Prophets—Reclaiming the Biblical Gifts* (Cleveland, OH: T.L. Lowery, 2004), 47.

[19]*Vine's Complete Expository Dictionary,* 493.

[20]Bill Hamon, *Prophets and the Prophetic Movement* (Shippensburg, PA: Destiny Image, 1990), 62.

[21]Webster's New Expanded Dictionary, 377.

[22]Lockyer, Hubert, *All the Women in the Bible.* (Grand Rapids, MI: Baker Books, 2000), 81.

[23]Linda Belleville, *Women Leaders and the Church: Three Critical Questions* (Grand Rapids, MI: Baker Books, 2000), 83.

CPSIA information can be obtained at www.ICGtesting.com
Printed in the USA
BVOW041521130712

295184BV00001B/30/P